THE CHINESE WAY TO KEEP FIT

This is a book
of gentle, effective
exercises designed to improve
circulation, correct poor posture, and
build muscle tone. The movements are based on
traditional martial arts practices that not only
offer physical benefits but also
strengthen the mind-body
connection.

Ideal for people just
starting an exercise program as
well as those recovering from or suffering
from a chronic illness. Literally anyone
can perform these exercises
and experience health
benefits—in as little as five minutes per day!

THE CHINESE WAY TO KEEP FIT

Traditional Chinese Movements for Health & Rejuvenation

Jiawen Miao

New Age Books

ISBN: 81-7822-124-1

First Indian Edition: Delhi, 2005

(Reprinted from *Simple Fitness Exercises: Traditional Chinese Movements for Health & Rejuvenation* published by Llewellyn Publications, U.S.A.)

© 2000 by Jiawen Miao

All rights reserved. No part of this publication may be reproduced or transmitted in any form or by any means, electronic or mechanical, including photocopying, recording, or by any information storage and retrieval system, without permission in writing from the publishers.

Disclaimer

The practices, techniques and stretches described in this book should not be used as an alternative to professional medical treatment. This book does not attempt to give any medical diagnosis, treatment, prescription, or suggestion for medication in relation to any human disease, pain, injury, deformity, or physical condition.
The author and publisher of this book are not responsible in any manner whatsoever for any injury which may occur through following the instructions contained herein. It is recommended that before beginning the stretches and techniques, you consult with your physician to determine whether you are medically, physically, and mentally fit to undertake this course of practice.

Published by
NEW AGE BOOKS
A-44 Naraina Phase-I
New Delhi-110 028 (INDIA)
Email: nab@vsnl.in
Website: www.newagebooksindia.com

For Sale in Indian Subcontinent Only

Printed in India
at Brijbasi Art Press Ltd.
E-46/11, Okhla Ind. Area, Ph-II,
New Delhi-110020

Contents

Preface ix
Introduction xi
    A Brief Introduction to Chinese
        Health-Enhancement Exercises xi
    Something to Know Before Learning the Exercises xii
    General Features of the Exercises in this Book xiv
    General Requirements of Exercising xiv

1   BREATHING EXERCISES 1

    Starting Position 2
    The Flying Bird 3
    Grasping the Cloud 4
    Popping Up and Down 6
    Arms Opening and Closing 8
    Playing with Waves 10
    The Walking Crane 12

2   SITTING EXERCISES 15

    Basic Sitting Method 16
    Swaying Torso in the Chi 17
    Swaying Head in the Chi 19

3 STANDING EXERCISES 21

General Requirements 22
The Preparation Pose 22
Form 1: Palms Pressed Together Pose 23
Form 2: Extended Arms Pose 25
Form 3: Propping Up Pose 26
Form 4: Pushing Down Pose 28
The Concluding Form 30

4 GENTLEMAN'S EIGHT-SECTION BROCADE 31

General Requirements 32
Starting Position 33
Form 1: Propping Up the Sky 34
Form 2: Drawing the Bow 36
Form 3: Raising One Hand 39
Form 4: Looking Back 42
Form 5: Clenching the Fists with Eyes Wide Open 45
Form 6: Pulling the Toes 47
Form 7: Swaying Head and Buttocks 50
Form 8: Jolting 52

5 WARRIOR'S EIGHT-SECTION BROCADE 55

General Requirements 56
The Preparation Pose 56
Form 1: Lifting the Earth and Propping Up the Sky 57
Form 2: Drawing the Bow 60
Form 3: Raising One Hand 63
Form 4: Looking Back 65
Form 5: Thrusting the Fists with Eyes Wide Open 67
Form 6: Swaying Head and Buttocks 69
Form 7: Pulling the Foot 71
Form 8: Bumping on the Horse 73
The Concluding Form 75

6 Stretching Exercises 77
Propping Up the Sky and Hugging the Earth 78
Lotus Waving Its Leaves 80
Pushing the Mountain Away 82
Showing the Way to the Fairyland 84
Looking Back at the Moon 86
Two Dragons into the Water 87
Mantis Ambushing 89
Leaves Falling Toward the Ground 91

7 Simple Tai Chi Forms 93
General Requirements 94
The Unpolarized Pose 96
Pressing Down the Chi 97
Driving the Monkey Away 99
Waving Hands in the Cloud 102
Playing with the Millstone 105

Conclusion *107*
Index *108*

Preface

Using this book, you can learn some traditional Chinese fitness exercises, including the Eight-Section Brocade and *Tai Chi Chuan*. Effectiveness for keeping fit, ease in learning, and economy of exercising time are the criteria for the exercises chosen in this book. It should be noted here that there is more to these exercises than first meets the eyes. Some people might think that these exercises are too simple and do not offer enough challenge. Actually, they require a tremendous amount of self-discipline.

You could say that dragon fighting is more advanced than bullfighting, but bullfighting is a lot easier and more useful than dragon fighting. Think about how many dragons you will meet in your lifetime, and how much effort you would have to make to master the skill of dragon fighting. The exercises offered here are simple, useful, and easy to master, like bullfighting. Hence, they are more suitable to the average person who is primarily interested in maintaining good health.

The general features of traditional Chinese fitness exercises are very different from some modern exercises such as aerobics or weightlifting. A concentration of the mind is always emphasized to reach a harmonic state between the spiritual mind and the physical body. The balance of *yin* and *yang,* the unity of man and environment, the integration of gesture with mind and *chi*—a Chinese word meaning "energy flow"—and the oneness of spirit with strength and momentum are just a few of these features.

In order for this to have any beneficial effect on your health, approaching it with confidence, sincerity, and perseverance in practicing the exercises is very important. Only with confidence can you develop sincerity and focus your mind while exercising; only with sincerity can you persevere to practice and gain the essence of the exercises; and only with perseverance can you get the beneficial effects of the exercises and develop more interest in them.

You are advised to practice at least once each day, three times for those who want to recover from a certain ailment, but never make yourself too tired exercising. Some of the exercises in this book need a certain amount of stretching and stress, but do not force yourself to go beyond the point of comfort.

Visualization is used in the text to help readers better understand the concepts presented. In most cases, when a mirrored action is to be followed, only the action to one side is illustrated in detail. Effort has been made to illustrate the movements of these exercises more with pictures than with words. However, it is suggested that you read the requirements for the exercises carefully and review them constantly to insure that you do the exercises correctly.

If this book succeeds in its goal of illustrating some effective and easy ways to learn traditional Chinese exercises, much of the credit should be given to Mr. Victor Devalcourt, who helped me a great deal with my English composition, Dr. Chang-Meng Hsiung, who provided me with much technical support, as well as Mr. Soegiharto Terta and Mr. Qihong Zhang, who helped me in taking the pictures. I would also like to express my special appreciation to Ms. Joanna Willis, the editor, for her patience and her careful examination of the book.

Introduction

A Brief Introduction to Chinese Health-Enhancement Exercises

In ancient years, the Chinese exercise for health enhancement was called *Daoyin*. Daoyin has a history as long as Chinese culture. In fact, there are so many different routines of Daoyin that nobody knows all of them. Despite the number of varieties of Daoyin, all of the exercises have the benefits of strengthening muscles, stretching tendons, and improving the function of joints and internal organs. What characterizes Daoyin is that it takes into consideration the overall balance of the physical body system and emphasizes the uniformity of the spiritual mind and the physical body.

Over the years, the Chinese people derived many different kinds of exercises from Daoyin and integrated some of them into Chinese martial arts. The exercises in this book are all related in some way to the fundamental practices of Chinese martial arts, or kung fu as some call it. As the practice of kung fu is very closely related to Chinese medical theory—consider yin and yang, the five elements, and the paths of chi flow—it is no wonder that each exercise has its special effect to cure a certain kind of illness.

Something to Know Before Learning the Exercises

Why people should exercise

Many people exert themselves in ways that might cause some physical problems. These exertions could be either physical or spiritual. Some people work at computers all day long and some have to stand all day by machines. Those who drive each day sit on seats with their hands on steering wheels for hours. Business people, who travel often, do not have a regular time to have their meals. All of these people suffer from certain tensions that cause fatigue. Fatigue can only be prevented or cured through exercising. Therefore, exercises are very important for a happy life and for maintaining efficiency.

What kinds of exercises are in this book

East Asian exercises are becoming increasingly popular in Western countries nowadays. Finding a good teacher is very important for learning these exercises. Unfortunately, teachers with both performing skills and teaching abilities are not available everywhere. Even if you have learned some exercises with a good teacher, it is still difficult to practice them perfectly and remember all the forms when practicing them later by yourself. This is why people have to learn or review the exercises using instruction books. Unfortunately, not every exercise is suitable for solitary learning. This is true especially for those traditional East Asian exercises that usually require an experienced teacher to learn from. On the other hand, many people in modern society want to benefit from exercise by practicing only a little. This is why I want to introduce the ideas of this book to you. The exercises introduced in this book are some simple, easy, effective, and time-saving practices. You can learn them without a teacher, you can do them without much physical strength or body flexibility, and you can practice them for only five minutes a day if you do not have much time for exercising. However, this does not mean that these exercises are less effective when compared to those that are more time-consuming and complicated.

Suggestions for learners

It is not suggested that you learn all the exercises in this book. Rather, you should choose your favorite exercises, those which are most suitable to you. Trying to do everything at the same time often results in accomplishing nothing. Before choosing the exercises in this book that are most appropriate for you, the following descriptions will be helpful in making your decision.

- Pregnant women and those with certain physical or mental problems should consult a doctor before doing the exercises in this book. For example, some exercises require bending down low. Such exercises are not suitable for people with hypertension or arteriosclerosis.

- The breathing methods introduced in chapter 1 are suitable for most people. It would be helpful to practice these exercises for a few weeks before practicing the other exercises in this book.

- The sitting exercises in chapter 2 are for those people who want to increase their overall internal physical balance. The second exercise, Swaying Torso in the Chi, is especially good for the digestive system.

- Chapters 3 and 5 are popular among martial arts practitioners. They are for those who want some advanced-level exercises. These exercises can strengthen your muscles and make your tendons more flexible.

- In chapter 4 the Eight-Section Brocade, an exercise for all ages and all professions, is introduced. It is especially recommended for people who work at desks every day. It is also one of my favorite exercises.

- Stretching exercises, which are introduced in chapter 6, can be used as warming-up exercises for various sports. They can be used as complementary exercises for Tai Chi Chuan because Tai Chi does not require a large extension of movement.

- Tai Chi Chuan has become increasingly popular in Western countries in recent years. The whole routine of Tai Chi is rather difficult to remember and usually takes a long time to learn. To meet the needs of those people who want to benefit from Tai Chi, some single forms are introduced in chapter 7. To repeat single forms is the primary stage before learning the whole routine. In fact, repeatedly practicing some single Tai Chi forms is more beneficial if a person's goal is health improvement.

- The exercises in chapters 3, 4, and 5 are usually considered whole routines. If you would like to practice only one or two of the forms, it is still necessary to start with the preparation form and finish with the concluding form.

- I do not suggest that you learn Yoga or some routines of Qigong at the same time as you are learning the exercises in this book, because you might mix up different exercises in this way. If you have learned Yoga or Qigong before, please do not mix up the exercise requirements. Do not apply the principles for a special exercise to other ones unless you have mastered them and are knowledgeable enough to do so.

- It is not advisable to practice the exercises in chapters 3, 4, 6, or 8 when one is feeling hungry, tired, exhilarated, or disturbed.

- Practicing twice a day is suggested. Practicing at least once daily is recommended. Practicing three times a day is advised for those who are recovering from a health problem.

General Features of the Exercises in this Book

The exercises in this book were designed both for internal and external strength. An overall balance was taken into consideration. So rather than emphasizing special muscles, every part of your organism can take part in the exercise. As one is practicing the exercises, both the breathing and the body movements are slow and the breathing is rhythmic and in harmony with the body movements. All of the exercises have been practiced for hundreds of years and are proven effective for maintaining health if they are practiced correctly.

General Requirements of Exercising

Wear loose clothes when you are preparing to do the exercises. Go to the bathroom before practicing. Find an open space with fresh air. Be relaxed both mentally and physically. You should have the sun at your back if you choose to stand under the sun. Your breathing should be deep and even. Breathe through your nose and no sound can be heard even by yourself. Always pay some attention, especially when you exhale, to your *dantian,* which is the internal point in your belly located one palm below your navel. Do not practice within one hour after a big meal or a half hour after a small meal.

Feel the sensations in your body during practice. Being comfortable is more important than mimicking the illustration pictures. Coordinate all parts of the body with your mind and breath. Apply the movements smoothly and gently. Exert consciousness rather than physical strength. When finishing an exercise, stand still with your attention on your dantian for a while and then massage your hands, head, lower abdomen, and other parts of your body before moving around.

1

Breathing Exercises

breathing is very important for almost all traditional Chinese health promotion exercises. A good breathing pattern is deep, smooth, and slow. Animals that breathe slowly, such as elephants and turtles, have longer lives than those who breathe quickly. A correct pattern of breathing is the basis for all of the exercises in this book. You do not have to practice all the breathing methods every time. Practicing one or two of them is recommended.

You are supposed to do the exercises slowly, gracefully, and in a relaxed manner. Exhaling usually takes a little longer than inhaling. There is usually a half-second interval during the inhale-exhale switch when you can adjust your breath a little, but body movement does not stop during this interval.

1.1   1.2

Starting Position

Stand with both feet parallel and shoulder-width apart as shown (photos 1.1 and 1.2). The weight of your body rests at the center. Relax your whole body with your arms hanging naturally by your sides. Relax all of your joints, but do not bend them intentionally. Look ahead, but pay attention to everything around you. Keep your head and neck erect while keeping your backbone straight. As a beginner you should also keep in mind that the tip of your nose corresponds to the navel and that your tailbone corresponds to the heels. With this image in mind, you automatically withdraw your chin and buttocks and relax your torso while keeping it erect.

Now breathe deeply, but do not hold it. Adjust your body a little to make yourself more comfortable. After you feel you have relaxed both physically and mentally, you can begin with the following forms.

Some common incorrect postures for beginners are protruding the chin, chest, or buttocks. Avoid shrugging your shoulders and just stand up straight and relax. You can ask a friend to check your posture in reference to the pictures in this book.

1.3 1.4

The Flying Bird

Begin with the Starting Position. Raise your arms from your sides to shoulder level while breathing in (photo 1.3). Lower your arms to the original position while breathing out (1.4). Move your hands slowly and softly like the tail of a fish. Repeat three to eight times.

This is the easiest exercise for coordinating your movement with your breath.

1.5

1.6

1.7

Grasping the Cloud

Begin with the Starting Position and look ahead. Lift your arms from both sides, with palms facing downward, and inhale at the same time (photo 1.5). When your hands reach the level of your forehead, turn the palms to face out (1.6). Then turn your palms to face each other while continuing to lift your hands until they are shoulder-width apart and your fingers point up. Imagine that you are grasping a white cloud while closing your hands. Now turn your hands with palms facing toward your head and stop for a half-second (1.7). Then, exhaling, lower your hands

Breathing Exercises

1.8   1.9

in front of you, palms facing down (1.8). Imagine that you are pushing the cloud into the ground through your body while you exhale (1.9). Let your hands return to your sides. When your hands reach their original place, stop the movement for a half-second. Repeat cyclically three to twelve times.

This exercise can help you relax both physically and mentally. It is also very helpful for those people who are suffering from hypertension, dizziness, or a tight chest. It is not suggested for people with hypotension or who are depressed. Do not protrude your chest or pull in your stomach when inhaling, and do not bow your head when exhaling. Always keep your torso straight.

1.10

Popping Up and Down

Begin with the Starting Position and look ahead. Lift your arms in front of your body with palms facing downward and inhale at the same time (photo 1.10). When your hands reach the level of your shoulder, switch your breath and exhale while your hands begin to press down (1.11). Bend your knees and lower your body a little (1.12). Continue to exhale and then press your hands down until they reach

1.11

Breathing Exercises

1.12

1.13

the level of your dantian (1.13). Reverse the movement and your breath to pop up. Repeat cyclically eight to thirty-six times. Imagine you are playing with a ball that is moving up and down in the water. Inhale while popping up and straightening your knees, exhale while pushing down and bending your knees.

This exercise is one of the basic exercises for Tai Chi learners. It helps you build up a breathing pattern that is rhythmic and in harmony with body movements. It is also an auxiliary therapeutic exercise for limb numbness and arthritis. Do not lean backward while inhaling or forward while exhaling. The arms and hands wave just like the tail of a fish. People who have arthritis in their knees can add the image of their knees holding a balloon. The balloon is so fragile that a little bit of pressure will break it. Keep the idea that the balloon will neither fall by releasing it nor break by pressing it.

1.14

Arms Opening and Closing

Begin with the Starting Position and then lift both arms in front of you to the level of your shoulders with your palms facing each other (photo 1.14). Separate the hands while inhaling to a distance of two shoulder-widths (1.15 and 1.16); close the hands while exhaling until they are one hand length apart (1.17). Keep your knees slightly bent

1.15

1.16 1.17

and your backbone straight so that your chest neither sags nor protrudes. Repeat the movement eight to thirty-six times.

This exercise is especially good for your respiratory system and your heart. Try to wave your arms like the tail of a fish. Imagine that there is a balloon between your hands. The balloon expands when you inhale and it contracts when you exhale. At the same time, the belly contracts while you open your hands and it expands while you close your hands.

1.18

Playing with Waves

Begin with the Starting Position. Inhale while lifting both arms sideways to shoulder level with palms facing forward (photo 1.18). Continue the arm movement with elbows bending and palms moving toward the ears (1.19). Then exhale while pushing the palms forward at shoulder level (1.20). Protrude the centers of your palms a little at the end of the pushing, but do not

1.19

I.20

exert your elbows. Turn the palms to face each other, lower the arms, and return to the original pose. Breathe in a little while lowering your arms. Repeat cyclically eight to thirty-six times.

    This exercise is good for your heart and lungs. It can also strengthen the tendons of your hands and arms. Remember, do not protrude your chest or pull in your lower back while lifting your arms. Also, do not lean forward while pushing.

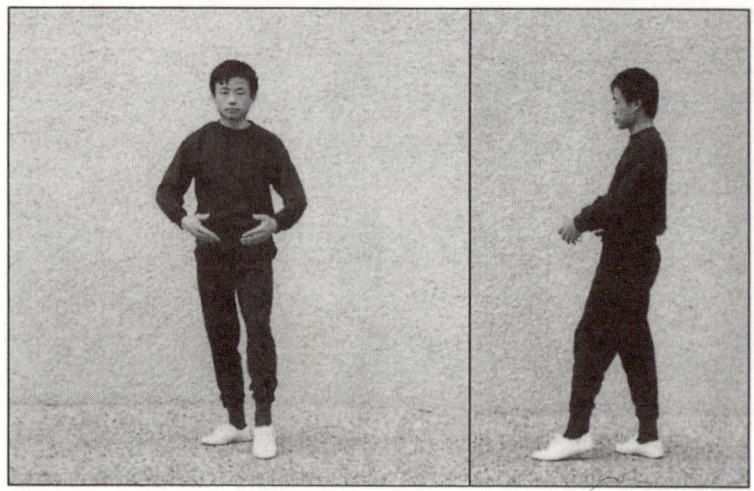

1.21

1.22

The Walking Crane

Walk slowly, two to eight steps per breath. Lift your arms in front of your body while gently drawing a deep breath. Your palms should face upward while lifting them from your dantian to your chest (photo 1.21). Continue lifting and turn your palms to face you as they pass from your chest to your forehead (1.22). Stretch your arms up and over your head to complete the motion, turning your palms to face

Breathing Exercises

1.23

1.24

1.25

upward as they pass your forehead (1.23). Then, while slowly exhaling, lower your arms sideways. Your palms should face outward while your arms lower from the top position to your head level (1.24) and they should face downward while your arms lower from head level to your thigh (1.25 and 1.26).

continued

1.26

This is a strolling exercise for when you are walking outside for some fresh air. The steps and the arm movements should be in rhythmic harmony with the breath. It is especially good for those suffering from hypotension or depression. People with hypertension, dizziness, or a headache are not advised to do this exercise.

2
Sitting Exercises

three exercises are introduced in this chapter. The first exercise is the foundation of almost all Chinese internal exercises. It will help you relax both your mind and body. Some people also use it as the basic pose for meditation. The second exercise in this chapter will help you stretch your spine and strengthen your digestive system. The third exercise can improve the condition of your neck muscles and ligaments.

2.1

Basic Sitting Method

Sit up straight on the edge of a bench (about four inches) with its height equal to that of your knees. Rest your hands on your knees with your feet flat on the ground and shoulder-width apart as shown (photo 2.1). Relax your shoulders while bending your elbows naturally. Draw in your chin and relax your chest. The tip of your nose is in line with your navel. Slightly close your eyes or look forward gently. Close your mouth and clench your teeth lightly. Rest the tip of your tongue on your palate as if you are going to pronounce "luh."

Breathe deeply and slowly; deeply, but do not hold your breath; slowly, but just to the extent that you feel uncomfortable. Calm down mentally and relax physically through this breathing pattern. Clear your mind while inhaling and relax your muscles while exhaling. Practice for five to fifteen minutes each time.

Sitting Exercises

2.2

2.3

2.4

2.5

Swaying Torso in the Chi

Begin with the Basic Sitting Method. Separate the feet to one and one-half shoulder widths apart (photo 2.2). Lean your torso to the right (2.3), forward in front (2.4), to the left side (2.5), backward a little (2.6–2.8), and then return to the right

continued

2.6

2.7

2.8

again. Exhale while bending forward and inhale while straightening the torso at the end of the cycle. Draw a circle like this thirty-six times. Return to the starting position and rest for one or two deep breaths. Then turn the torso in the opposite direction for thirty-six times. Imaging that your torso is swaying in an ocean of chi. Take two to six deep breaths before finishing. This exercise takes fifteen to twenty minutes.

This exercise is for overall balance of the internal organs. It is especially helpful for recovering from poor digestion, poor bowel movement, lumbago, and insomnia.

Sitting Exercises

2.9

2.10

2.11

2.12

Swaying Head in the Chi

Sit in the posture of the Basic Sitting Method described on page 16 (photo 2.9). As you turn your head, keep your trunk still. Lean your head to one side and look at your shoulder (2.10). Continue the rotation and look at your stomach as your head inclines forward (2.11). Follow the progression of photos 2.12 and 2.13 and as

continued

2.13

2.14

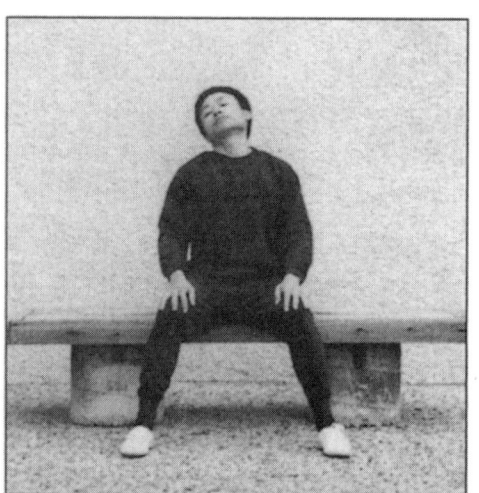

2.15

your head inclines backward, look up (2.14 and 2.15). Turn your head in each direction twelve times. Exhale while bending your head down and inhale while lifting it.

This exercise is especially good for people who work at computers for long hours. It helps relieve fatigue of the neck and eyes.

3

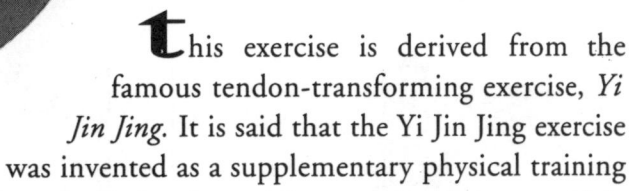

Standing Exercises

This exercise is derived from the famous tendon-transforming exercise, *Yi Jin Jing*. It is said that the Yi Jin Jing exercise was invented as a supplementary physical training for those monks who meditated all day long. The exercise is now widely accepted as a basic training by Shaolin school martial arts practitioners. The traditional Yi Jin Jing is a time-consuming twelve-form exercise, and it is difficult to learn without the correct instruction of a good master. The four-form exercise introduced in this book is a simplified version that needs less time to practice and can be learned from a book. To practice this exercise, it is suggested that you schedule a fifteen- to forty-five-minute period and find a place where nobody will disturb you.

General Requirements

- Breathe evenly and slowly through your nose.
- Close your mouth, teeth clenched slightly.
- Keep your backbone straight without protruding or withdrawing any part of your trunk.
- Always pay some attention to your dantian, that is, the point one palm-width below your navel.

The Preparation Pose

Stand at ease with your feet parallel to each other and shoulder-width apart as shown (photos 3.1 and 3.2). Relax physically, but keep an alert mind. Let your hands hang naturally by your sides with your knees slightly bent. Withdraw your chin, chest, and buttocks to keep your torso straight. Close your teeth and mouth lightly and breathe evenly through your nose. Look ahead, but pay some attention to your entire body. Clear your mind and concentrate on the exercise.

3.1   3.2

3.3

3.4

3.5

Form 1: Palms Pressed Together Pose

Lift both arms slowly at 45-degree angles to your body to ear height and breathe in (photo 3.3). Slowly bring your hands together (3.4), press your palms together and with your fingers pointing toward your throat, breathe out (3.5 and 3.6). Keep the first digits of your fingers and the heels of your palms touching each other. Your fingertips are about three inches away from

continued

3.6

your throat. Look ahead calmly, but pay attention to your entire body. Remember the image of the tip of your nose corresponding to your navel. Hold this pose for five to fifteen minutes before moving on to the next pose.

This form helps you concentrate and is especially good for the lungs and respiratory system.

3.7

3.8

3.9

3.10

Form 2: Extended Arms Pose

From the last pose separate your palms and with your fingers still pointed to each other, press your hands down toward your dantian while exhaling (photo 3.7). Lower your hands to your sides and then raise your arms sideways to the level of your shoulders while inhaling, palms facing downward (3.8–3.10). Keep this pose and breathe gently as long as you can. Your eyes should be wide open. Pay some attention both to the centers of your hands and the centers of your feet. Hold this pose as long as you can until you feel your arms getting tired.

This form helps you sense the uniformity of the body and the mind.

3.11

3.12

Form 3: Propping Up Pose

From the last pose turn your palms upward and raise your arms above your head until your fingers are pointing upward (photos 3.11 and 3.12). Then turn your hands, palms facing upward and fingers pointed to each other (3.13 and 3.14). The above movement is accompanied by an inhalation. Look upward through the fingers and stretch your arms a little. Try to keep the backbone straight and relaxed.

3.13 **3.14**

Hold the position as long as you can and breathe gently through your nose. Pay a little more attention to the centers of your palms while you are breathing in. Pay a little more attention to the centers of your feet while you are breathing out. Rest the tip of your tongue on the palate. Grasp the ground with your toes and lift the heels a little if you can stay balanced. Hold this pose as long as you can until you feel your arms getting tired.

This form helps to strengthen the whole body and create a tranquil mind.

3.15

3.16

3.17

Form 4: Pushing Down Pose

From the last pose relax and exhale while pushing your hands downward in front of you (photos 3.15 and 3.16). Continue to bend downward as far as you can and interlock your fingers while you reach for the ground. Lift your head, eyes looking ahead and body bent downward (3.17 and 3.18).

3.18

Pay some attention to the tip of your nose and the center of your hands. Hold the position with your hands as close to the ground as you can, but do not bend your knees. Your eyes are wide open and your teeth are clenched tightly. Keep the position as long as you can and breathe naturally.

This form helps strengthen the back.

3.19

3.20

3.21

3.22

The Concluding Form

Return to the starting pose for awhile. Bending your knees, jolt up and down (photos 3.19 and 3.20) and wriggle your torso (3.21 and 3.22). Try to relax all the muscles while jolting and wriggling. The muscles and internal organs can be gently shaken in this way. Stand still for a while and take a few deep breaths. Massage your hands, head, and abdomen before you move.

4

Gentleman's Eight-Section Brocade

This traditional exercise has been in existence for more than eight hundred years. Because of its effectiveness for keeping fit, it was accepted by Shaolin monks as one of the basic entry-level exercises for the Shaolin *wushu*, or martial art. The Eight-Section Brocade is an ideal lifetime exercise for most people. Regular practice of this exercise can strengthen one's internal organs as well as one's muscles and tendons. Stretching coordinated with breathing is characteristic of the Eight-Section Brocade.

General Requirements

- Practice the whole routine every day at a regular time and exercise one or two of the forms whenever you feel it would be beneficial.
- Do not exercise within an hour after meals.
- Practice in a place where the space is large, the scene is delightful, and the air is fresh.
- Take a few deep breaths before beginning the routine.
- Be relaxed both mentally and physically.
- Your breaths and movements should be even, slow, and natural.
- Stretch your tendons through gentle exertion.
- Concentrate your attention on your dantian when exhaling.
- Stop for a half-second after each inhalation or exhalation.
- Relax yourself and walk around for a while after practicing.
- Repeat each form two to eight times. It takes five to twenty minutes for the whole routine.

Gentleman's Eight-Section Brocade

4.1 **4.2**

Starting Position

Stand comfortably with your hands hanging by your thighs and your feet shoulder-width apart as shown (photos 4.1 and 4.2). Draw in your chin, belly, and buttocks to keep your torso straight. Relax totally and breathe naturally through your nose. Look ahead and close your mouth and teeth lightly with the tongue resting on the palate. Focus your mind and pay a little attention to your dantian.

4.3

4.4 **4.5**

Form 1: Propping Up the Sky

Raise your hands in front of your body with your palms facing upward (photo 4.3). Turn your palms to face you when they pass by your face (4.4). Continue the movement and turn your palms outward and up as you stretch your arms and whole body upward (4.5). Look up and lift your heels while stretching (4.6). Return to the start-

4.6

4.7   **4.8**

ing pose by lowering your arms sideways with your heels on the ground (4.7 and 4.8). Inhale while lifting your hands and exhale while lowering them.

    This form can relieve fatigue and eliminate weariness. It also helps to rebuild an erect posture of the chest and back. With the help of propping upward, you can breathe in more fresh air. While stretching your muscles, ligaments, and bones, this form also stimulates the internal organs.

Form 2: Drawing the Bow

Take a big side step with your feet two shoulder-widths apart and arms crossed (photo 4.9). Lift your hands, forearms crossed, right arm on top (4.10). Stretch out your left arm in front of you, palm facing out, with your index and middle fingers erect and your other fingers bent; bend the right arm while making a fist and draw your elbow back and to the right

4.9

4.10

side (4.11 and 4.12). Then bend your knees further as if riding on a horse and spread out your arms further as if drawing a bow with power. Draw a half-circle with your right hand and spread out both arms as shown in photo 4.13. Then lower your arms, relax, and stand up straight (4.14). Repeat this movement with the other side. Inhale when drawing the bow and exhale when returning to the starting pose. Remember to keep your

4.11

4.12

continued

4.13 **4.14**

weight centered on the middle and to not protrude your buttocks while drawing the bow.

This form can enhance the functions of the respiratory and circulatory systems. Practicing this form can strengthen the muscles of the hands, arms, chest, and thighs.

4.15

4.16

4.17

Form 3: Raising One Hand

Start with a small step sideways, standing straight in a relaxed way. Lift your hands to your stomach with your palms facing upward (photo 4.15). Continue the movement by lifting the left hand up and pressing the right hand down (4.16). Turn your palms so that the left hand ends facing up and the right hand ends facing down (4.17). Remember to keep your arms vertical, your left hand

continued

4.18

4.19

pointing to the right, and your right hand pointing forward while stretching your arms (4.18). Return to the starting pose by lowering your left hand in front of your body (4.19 and 4.20). Reverse the action by lifting the right hand. Inhale while lifting your arm and exhale while lowering it.

4.20

By pulling your two arms in opposite ways, your internal organs and muscles are stretched. This exercise can strengthen the digestive system as well as the muscles in the arms and shoulders.

4.21

4.22

Form 4: Looking Back

Start with a small step sideways. Look ahead with your body relaxed. Lift your left arm around the front of your face and hug the back of your head. At the same time, reach your right hand in back of you and touch your back with the back of your hand as far up as is comfortable (photos 4.21 and 4.22). Then clench the right ear with the index and middle fingers of your

Gentleman's Eight-Section Brocade

4.23

4.24

left hand. Turn your waist to the right and look at the left heel (4.23 and 4.24). Return to the starting pose, lowering the left hand around your neck (4.25 and 4.26). Reverse this movement. Inhale while lifting your arms and turning your waist. Exhale while returning to the starting pose. Keep your body up straight while looking back.

This form is believed to relieve fatigue caused by holding a particular

continued

4.25

4.26

position or being overcome by a certain mood for a long period of time. The exercise helps to strengthen the muscles of the neck and around the eye sockets. It also stimulates the central nervous system and prevents fatigue of the cervical vertebrae.

4.27

4.28 **4.29**

Form 5: Clenching the Fists with Eyes Wide Open

Take a big step sideways, feet parallel and at two shoulder-widths apart. Bend your knees and drop your torso with your fists beside your waist (photo 4.27). Punch a fist slowly forward using internal force, a gentle exertion (4.28–4.30). Turn the

continued

4.30

4.31

4.32

hand and then withdraw the fist (4.31 and 4.32). Punch two fists in turn. Inhale when withdrawing the fist and exhale when punching. Teeth are clenched tightly and eyes opened wide as if you were angry. Toes should grip the ground firmly. Do not protrude the buttocks or pull in the lower back.

This form helps to improve muscular strength and stamina. It also promotes blood circulation and stimulates the nervous system. The angry eyes and the tightly clenched fists are very important for the effectiveness of this form.

4.33

4.34

4.35

Form 6: Pulling the Toes

Stand at ease (photo 4.33). Lift your arms in front and reach overhead (4.34 and 4.35). With your knees bent a little, lean backward as shown in photo 4.36. Then, with your hands still in the air, bend forward and try to grasp your toes with your hands (4.37). Pull your toes and keep your legs straight (4.38). Inhale while leaning backward and exhale while bending down. If you are

continued

4.36

4.37

not limber enough to reach your toes, just stretch the arms toward the ground as far as you can.

This practice helps to flatten the stomach, strengthen the back, and adjust the spine. By stretching the front and the back of your body cyclically, it is also good for the organs in your belly.

Gentleman's Eight-Section Brocade

4.38

4.39

4.40

4.41

4.42

Form 7: Swaying Head and Buttocks

Take a big step sideways and bend down. Let your arms hang naturally (photo 4.39). The first movement is raising and lowering the two shoulders in turn to swivel the vertebrae of the spine (4.40–4.42). The second movement is swinging

4.43

4.44

the two hands back and forth in opposite ways while swaying the head and hips right and left (4.43 and 4.44). The spine weaves like a snake at the same time. Breathe naturally. All the movements should be done in a relaxed way.

This is a relaxation exercise for relieving tension in the nervous system and for adjusting the spine.

Form 8: Jolting

Stand at ease as shown in photo 4.45. Lift your heels and raise your body (4.46). Then lower your heels suddenly. Follow through by raising your toes and flexing your ankles (4.47). This gives your body a little shock. Inhale while lifting the heels and exhale while lowering them. For those who are not very strong, lower the

4.45

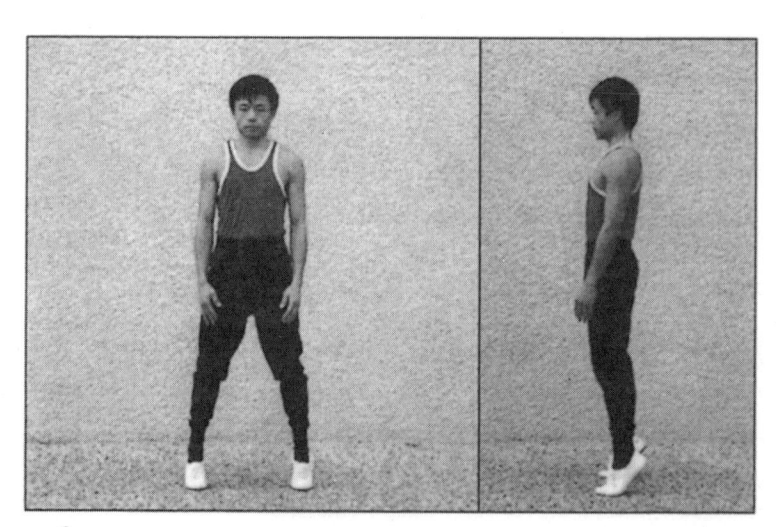

4.46

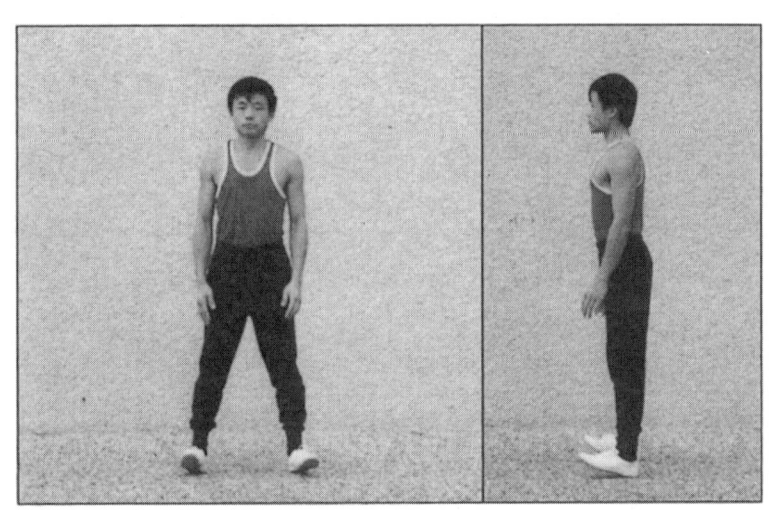

4·47

heels gently instead of suddenly. The head should be kept erect to prevent too much shock to the cervical vertebrae.

This form serves as the closing form by applying some light vibration to the spine and internal organs. It also helps to strengthen the ligaments along the spine and has certain therapeutic effects for flat feet.

5

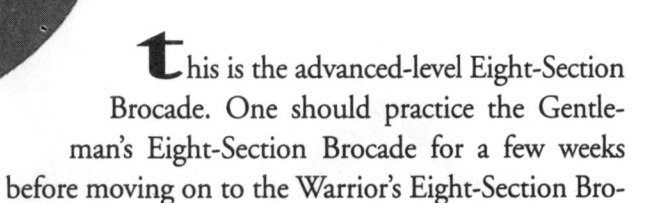

Warrior's Eight-Section Brocade

This is the advanced-level Eight-Section Brocade. One should practice the Gentleman's Eight-Section Brocade for a few weeks before moving on to the Warrior's Eight-Section Brocade. Regular practice of this exercise can increase one's stamina and power. For other benefits of this exercise, please refer to the corresponding forms of the Gentleman's Eight-Section Brocade. If you are practicing it for health, a ten-minute routine each time is enough. If you are practicing it for martial arts training, you should do it for at least a half hour each time.

General Requirements

It should be noted that the breathing in most forms here are just reversed when compared to the Gentleman's Eight-Section Brocade. The stretching movements should be done with extreme internal force and accompanied by exhaling. The toes should grip the ground firmly and the fingers should be clenched tightly when fists are used. Clench the teeth tightly and open the eyes wide when internal force is exerted. Because this routine requires intense exertion, I would suggest doing some warm-up stretches or five minutes of the Gentleman's Eight-Section Brocade before beginning the Warrior's Eight-Section Brocade.

The Preparation Pose

Take an "on-the-horse step" with your fists loose at both sides, as shown in photo 5.1. Breathe calmly and focus your mind on your dantian. Every one of the following forms should begin with this pose.

5.1

5.2

5.3

5.4

5.5

Form 1: Lifting the Earth and Propping Up the Sky

Begin with the Preparation Pose (5.1). Lift your hands overhead and then press them down in front of you to the ground (photos 5.2–5.4). Straighten your knees in this movement. Inhale while lifting your hands and exhale while pressing down. Then, turn your hands outward and make fists (5.5). Take a horse-riding

continued

5.6

5.7

stance and drop your torso as shown in photo 5.6. With your knees still bent, stand up a little and lift your fists from the ground as shown in photo 5.7. Using internal force or gentle exertion, stretch your hands upward and overhead and straighten your torso while dropping the body a little at the same time (5.8). Then

5.8

5.9

slowly straighten your knees and stand up straight. Lower your arms to their original position (5.9). Inhale while lifting the fists and exhale while stretching upward. Repeat cyclically eight to sixteen times. Lift the fists as if you were lifting the earth. Stretch upward as if you were supporting the sky.

Form 2: Drawing the Bow

Begin with the Preparation Pose (5.1). Cross your arms and stand as shown in photo 5.10. Lift both fists in front of your chest (5.11). Extend your left arm out in front of you and bend your right elbow back (5.12). Stretch your left arm and right elbow in opposite directions and drop your body as if drawing a bow on horseback (5.13).

continued on page 62

5.10

5.11

5.12

5.13

5.14 **5.15**

Inhale while lifting your fists and exhale while drawing the bow. Draw a half-circle with your right hand and spread out both arms as shown in photo 5.14. Then lower your arms, relax, and stand up straight (5.15). Reverse the movement by drawing the bow to the right. Repeat cyclically eight to sixteen times.

5.16

5.17

5.18

Form 3: Raising One Hand

Begin with the Preparation Pose. Lift your left hand with your palm toward your face (photo 5.16). Swivel your torso to the right with your right knee bent and the other knee straight (5.17). Bend down and draw a big arc with your left hand (5.18 and 5.19). Finish the arc, lift up your body, and lift your left hand to face level (5.20).

continued

5.19

5.20

5.21

Facing left, stretch your arms at a slant, one palm up and the other down (5.21). Return to the original pose and reverse the movement. Inhale while turning to the right and lifting the left hand. Exhale while bending down and stretching the arms. Repeat cyclically eight to sixteen times.

5.22

5.23

5.24

Form 4: Looking Back

Begin with the Preparation Pose. Lift both hands to chest level (photo 5.22) and turn your waist to the right (5.23). Push your hands at a slant in opposite directions while you slightly bend your right knee and straighten your left knee (5.24). Look back at

continued

5.25

5.26

your left heel while pushing the hands. Lower your arms, return to the original stance and reverse the movement (5.25 and 5.26). Inhale while lifting your hands to chest level and exhale while looking back.

5.27

5.28

5.29

Form 5: Thrusting the Fists with Eyes Wide Open

Begin with the Preparation Pose. Lower your body with your fists by your waist (photo 5.27). While applying extreme internal force or exertion, slowly punch out both fists, then withdraw them. Follow the progression of photos 5.28–5.32.

continued

5.30

5.31

5.32

Imagine you are pushing a mountain while punching and you are stopping a running horse while withdrawing the fists. Inhale while withdrawing the fists and exhale while punching.

Form 6: Swaying Head and Buttocks

Begin with the Preparation Pose. Straighten your legs and grasp your ankles with both hands as shown in photo 5.33. Sway your head to the right and your buttocks to the left suddenly (5.34). Exhale while making

continued

the sudden move and inhale while returning to center (5.35). Do the same thing in the opposite direction (5.36). Repeat cyclically eight to sixteen times.

5.35

5.36

5.37

Form 7: Pulling the Foot

From the Preparation Pose, stand as shown in photo 5.37 with your feet at 45-degree angles to each other. Lift your right leg and hold your foot with both hands (5.38). Stretch the lifted

5.38

continued

5.39

5.40

leg out, keeping both legs straight (5.39). Inhale while withdrawing the foot, with hands holding it, and exhale while stretching out the leg. Return to the original stance (5.40). Repeat on each side for three to nine times.

5.41

5.42

Form 8: Bumping on the Horse

Lift your hands sideways, palms facing up and legs straight (photo 5.41). Press your hands down, drop your torso to knee level and lift your heels (5.42). Inhale as you stand up again (5.43 and 5.44) and exhale as you squat down. Repeat the

continued

5.43　　　　　　　　　**5.44**

movement many times. Imagine that you are lifting two heavy iron balls while you are lifting your hands. Imagine that you are pressing two big balloons into the water while squatting.

5.45

The Concluding Form

Finish the routine by holding your palms on your dantian as shown (photo 5.45).

6

Stretching Exercises

these exercises can serve as preparation exercises for more intense sports or they can complement the practice of Tai Chi. People who maintain a certain posture for a long time will also find that the exercises help to relieve fatigue. By practicing the stretching exercises, all of the joints, ligaments, and muscles in your body take part in the practice and hence benefit from it.

The movements should be done slowly and smoothly using internal force and slow and gentle exertions, usually one movement cycle for each breath. Begin with small movements and gradually apply more tension to your ligaments. You should be able to feel tension and tightness in your muscles while stretching. The intensity of exercising and the number of repeats should be increased gradually. Control the repetitions so you feel neither overworked nor bored. Coordinate the movements with your breathing, but never hold your breath.

Propping Up the Sky and Hugging the Earth

Lift your hands in front of your body with fingertips touching and palms facing upward (photo 6.1). Lift your arms up overhead, palms facing up, and stretch your whole body (6.2). Then lower your hands sideways with your palms downward (6.3). Bend your body down and flex your waist as

6.1

6.2

Stretching Exercises

much as you can (6.4). With your hands make a scooping-up motion and lift your body up. Repeat several times. Inhale while making the propping pose and exhale while bending down.

6.3

6.4

6.5

6.6

6.7

Lotus Waving Its Leaves

Place your forearms horizontally in front of your chest, with your left hand pointing to the right on the top and your right hand pointing to the left below it (photo 6.5). In one continuous motion, spread your arms sideways, turn your palms upward, and turn your waist to the left (6.6). Stretch out your arms and fingers with the thumbs wide open. Look backward (6.7). Return to the original pose

Stretching Exercises

6.8

6.9

6.10

with the right arm on the top (6.8). Do the same thing to the right (6.9 and 6.10). Inhale while stretching the arms and exhale while retracting them. Repeat the cycle several times.

Pushing the Mountain Away

Take a big step sideways, with your feet two shoulder-widths apart (photo 6.11). Raise your arms sideways and, bending your elbows, bring your hands close to your ears (6.12 and 6.13). Push your hands outward, thumbs opening wide and pointing

6.11

6.12

downward. Bend your knees and drop your trunk while pushing your hands outward (6.14). Inhale while raising your arms and exhale while pushing your hands outward. Lower your arms, lift your torso (6.11), and repeat several times.

6.13

6.14

6.15

6.16

Showing the Way to the Fairyland

Step sideways with your feet two shoulder-widths apart. Bend your elbows and lift your palms to your side (photo 6.15). Stretch your fingers and open your thumbs wide. Twist to the left and stick out your right hand with your thumbs pointed up and your left knee slightly bent (6.16 and

Stretching Exercises

6.17

6.17). Return to the original pose and do the same thing to the right. Inhale while drawing your hands to the sides of your chest and exhale while sticking out one hand. Repeat cyclically several times.

6.18

6.19

6.20

Looking Back at the Moon

Take a big step with your feet two shoulder-widths apart. Position your two hands beside your waist and be prepared to stretch (photo 6.18). Swivel your torso and bend down to reach your right ankle with your left hand (6.19). Hold the ankle firmly and lift your right hand. Keep your knees straight while looking back at your right hand (6.20). Return to the original pose and then do the same thing to the left. Inhale while positioning your hands by your waist and exhale while bending down. Repeat cyclically several times.

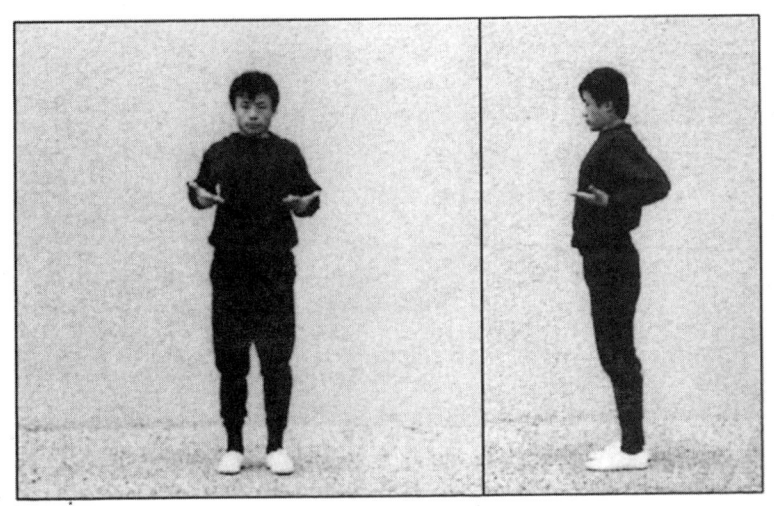

6.21

6.22

Two Dragons into the Water

Stand up straight with your feet one foot's-width apart. Bend your elbows and turn your palms upward on the side of your chest, fingers stretched and thumbs opened wide (photo 6.21). Twist your wrists and thrust out both hands, thumbs pointing up (6.22). Squat low to the ground while

continued

6.23

stretching your arms, feet flat on the ground (6.23). Inhale while drawing the hands and standing up, and exhale while thrusting the hands and squatting. Repeat the movement several times.

6.24

6.25

Mantis Ambushing

Take a big bow step sideways, right leg bent and left leg straight, with your feet two and one-half shoulder-widths apart and your hands facing upward by your chest (photo 6.24). Draw your two elbows backward, then bend your right knee and drop your buttocks while lifting your arms overhead, palms facing upward (6.25). Stretch your fingers, arms, and torso and look up while dropping the buttocks a little

continued

6.26

more toward the ground (6.26). While stretching, keep your thumbs open wide and pointing forward. The other fingers should be pointing at each other. Return to the original pose and do the same thing to the left. Inhale while lifting your arms and exhale while lowering them. Repeat cyclically several times.

6.27

6.28

6.29

6.30

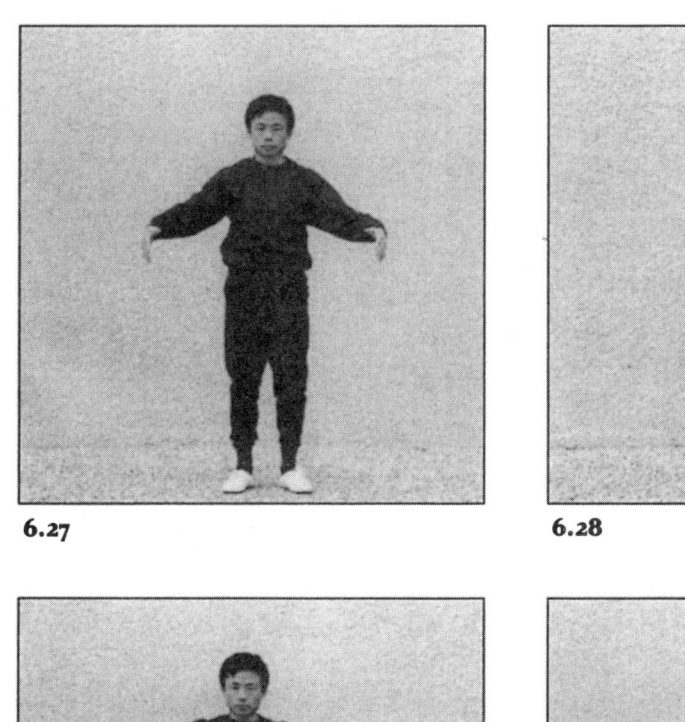

Leaves Falling Toward the Ground

Lift your arms sideways as high as you can (photos 6.27 and 6.28). Then press your hands down along the side of your body (6.29 and 6.30). Inhale while lifting your arms and exhale while lowering them. This is a relaxation exercise rather than a stretching one. It serves as the concluding form for the whole routine. Repeat several times before you finish.

7
Simple Tai Chi Forms

tai Chi Chuan, also known to westerners as *Tai Chi,* is an exercise with the movements of one's head, eyes, arms, hands, body, legs, and feet done in coordination with one's mind and respiration. People describe Tai Chi practice as "flying clouds and flowing streams." Phrases like "exerting strength like pulling silk threads from a cocoon," "hiding the power as a needle in cotton," and "concentrating one's spirit inwardly while appearing peaceful outwardly" are also frequently cited.

There are five secrets for Tai Chi practice. The first secret is the tranquillity of the mind. This tranquillity is the basis for concentration and alertness. Another secret is that the body should always be relaxed and agile. This results in apparent peacefulness and gracefulness. Other secrets include gathering the chi to penetrate the entire body, unifying the strength of the whole body, and developing the chi into spirit.

The correct way to master the art of Tai Chi is to begin with the practice of a stationary posture and of some simple repeated exercises. In fact, the whole routine of Tai Chi is usually difficult to remember. It requires years of supervised instruction with a master to become proficient at it. If one is just learning Tai Chi for health purposes, but not for its value as a martial art, practicing some simple Tai Chi forms repeatedly will be enough for one's physical well-being. This is the purpose for introducing some of the Tai Chi forms in this chapter.

The first form in this chapter, the Unpolarized Pose, is the essential exercise for mastering the essence of the five secrets mentioned above. The second form, Pressing Down the Chi, helps you to sink the chi into your dantian and to build a correct pattern of breathing. The third, fourth, and fifth forms are exercises for the coordination of mind, sight, and body movement. When practicing the last three forms one should be aware that the legs are the base and the waist is the axis. The mind directs the sight and the hands follow the sight. The whole body is in constant motion.

General Requirements

Correct postures are very important for Tai Chi practice. There are five basic requirements for the head and ten for the body to keep a correct posture. The five basic requirements for the head are:

1. suspending the head by an imaginary string from above
2. relaxing the neck, but keeping it erect
3. drawing in the chin slightly
4. closing the mouth and clenching the teeth slightly with the tongue touching the front palate, like pronouncing "luh"
5. looking forward, but hiding one's spirit behind the eyes; or, concentrating one's spirit inwardly while appearing peaceful outwardly

The ten basic requirements for body postures are:

1. releasing the tension in the chest
2. lifting the back

3. relaxing the shoulders
4. dropping the elbows
5. opening the arm pits
6. not protruding the stomach
7. centering the tailbone as if it were hanging
8. keeping a rounded space between the legs
9. bending the knees to protect the crotch
10. sinking the chi into your dantian

In addition to the above requirements, five imaginary correlations are also very important to keep a correct posture. With these five imaginary correlations, the movements of different parts of the body will be more coordinated, like a well-organized machine. The five imaginary correlations are:

1. the tip of the nose corresponds to the navel
2. the tailbone corresponds to the heels
3. the middle fingers correspond to each other
4. the knees correspond to the big toes of the feet
5. the elbows correspond to the knees

The mind should always concentrate on the movements you are performing. The breathing should be in rhythmic harmony with your body movements. Your body movements should be slow, soft, and graceful. They should be slow but not interrupted, soft but not slack, graceful but not weak. A very slow and circular movement is especially important for beginners, but the slow speed should only be to the extent that you can breathe naturally and coordinately. Only with this kind of slow movement can you concentrate on the details. A smooth and constant pace will help you get the real feeling of Tai Chi.

Not only are Tai Chi movements in a circular pattern, the gestures are also circular in form. In other words, there are no convex or concave movements. The spine, the arms, the fingers, and the legs are all like bows. Be alert, but with no unnecessary tension. That is where the momentum comes from.

All of the above requirements can be summarized as being like a full ball. Try to get this feeling while you practice.

7.1

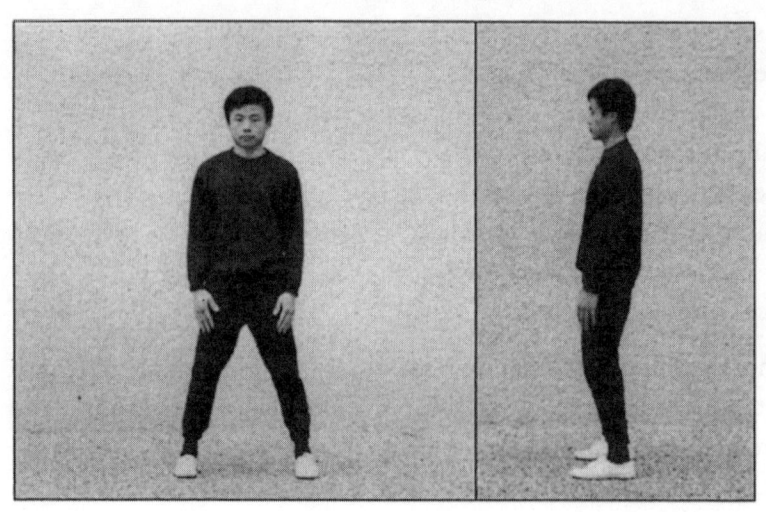

The Unpolarized Pose

Stand straight with your feet shoulder-width apart as shown in photo 7.1. Relax all your joints, but do not intentionally bend any of them. Hold your head erect and drop your shoulders to loosen the neck and back. Let your arms hang naturally with your palms facing your thighs. Draw in your chin, chest, belly, and buttocks to keep the backbone straight. Straighten your legs while keeping your knees flexed. Close your lips and teeth gently with the tip of your tongue resting on the palate near the teeth. Your eyes are either looking forward or are slightly closed. While paying attention to your whole body and the space around your body, focus more attention on your dantian. Breathe deeply, evenly, and slowly through the nose. Pull in your lower abdomen while breathing in and extend it while breathing out. The feeling of expansion should spread to your whole body as you get more experience with the exercises.

It would be helpful for beginners to keep the head up and the spine straight with the image of the nose corresponding to the navel and the tailbone corresponding to the heels.

Begin with a five-minute daily practice. Then it is recommended that you advance to two fifteen- to thirty-minute practices every day. This exercise has a therapeutic effect on the nervous system and internal organs.

7.2

7.3

7.4

Pressing Down the Chi

Begin with the Unpolarized Pose. Raise your arms forward at an angle to eye level, palms facing downward (photo 7.2). Then, while continuing to raise the hands a little higher than the head, turn your palms gradually to face each other. Palms and fingers should slant upward (7.3). Imagine that you are touching the surface of a big ball. Continue the movement by turning the palms downward. Then lower your hands to the level of your dantian, your fingers pointing toward each other (7.4 and 7.5).

continued

7.5

Breathe in while raising your arms and breathe out while lowering them. Remember to relax the shoulders and drop the elbows while raising the arms. You can feel the chi filling your dantian while you are lowering your hands in front of your body. Repeat the movement many times.

7.6

7.7

7.8

Driving the Monkey Away

Begin with a pose like you are holding a ball in front of your chest, with your knees and elbows bent (photo 7.6). Turn your palms to face upward. Then draw your right hand to the side of your waist and turn your waist a little to the right (7.7). Continue to turn your waist and lift your right hand up to the side of your ear (7.8

continued

and 7.9). Push your right hand forward and draw your left hand to the side of your waist while turning your waist to the left (7.10). Slightly protrude your shoulder and the center of your right palm when your palm nears the end of its path. Follow through as shown in photo 7.11 and reverse the movements using the left hand (7.12 and 7.13).

7.9

7.10

7.11

7.12

7.13

Repeat cyclically many times. Breathe in while swirling the arm and breathe out while driving the hand outward. Your hands should move in circular paths. Remember to relax your shoulders and drop your elbows while swirling up. Try to feel the resistance of the air with the pushing hand. You can either look forward or let your sight lead the hand that is swirling and driving out.

7.14

7.15

7.16

7.17

Waving Hands in the Cloud

Begin with your right hand in front of your face and your left hand in front of your navel (photo 7.14). Your knees are bent and your feet are shoulder-width apart. Keep your upper hand facing your body like you are holding a balloon and turn the wrist of your lower hand so that your palm faces the ground as if it were resting on a floating balloon. Now move both hands so that they are drawing vertical circles in opposite directions. To do this, lower the upper hand on the outside, palm facing

7.18

7.19

7.20

out and then down, and lift the lower hand on the inside, palm facing in. When the upper hand and lower hand are switching positions, the descending hand faces outward and the rising hand faces inward as if they were taking the balloons from the other hand. At the same time your hands are moving, pivot your torso, keeping your feet pointed forward as shown. When your hands switch positions, your torso should be coming to the end of its path, facing sideways and switching directions. Follow the progression of photos (7.15–7.22).

continued

7.21

7.22

Breathe in while switching the upper and lower hands, breathe out while pivoting. Do not lift your shoulder when you lift your hand. Your palms should move in circular paths. Your fingers should always be bent a little, with the center of the palms curved slightly inward. Your sight should lead the upper hand while you are waving it in front of your face.

7.23

7.24

Playing with the Millstone

Take a stable bow step with your front knee bent and your back knee straight. Your front foot is turned slightly inward and your rear foot is turned sideways at a 45-degree angle. Now draw a horizontal circle at navel level with both hands. Begin the circle with your hands near your belly and continue the movement in

continued

7.25

7.26

cycles. Let your trunk follow your hands and draw circles at the same pace. Follow the progression of photos 7.23–7.26.

Imagine your hands are resting on a floating balloon. The weight of your body is just like liquid flowing from one leg to the other as you shift your weight. Keep your tailbone pointing toward the ground and imagine your head is elevated like a balloon. Look at the space between your hands. Do not protrude your front knee over the vertical line from your front toe. Pay no attention to when you should breathe in or out since you can adjust the speed of the circular movement, but keep the speed of breathing regular.

Conclusion

I hope you have enjoyed learning the exercises in this book and have benefited from them. Though several different routines have been introduced here, you do not have to learn or practice all of them. Learn the exercises one by one and do not begin the next one until you are sophisticated with the first one. Mimic the body movements first and then try to coordinate your respiration with the body movements. Gradually you will be able to relax and focus more on your visualization as you become sophisticated with the body movements. Just choose one or two of the exercises which you like the most for your daily routine. For the purposes of mastering the essence of the exercises, you need to read through the text carefully and review the book constantly.

Since all of the exercises here have been nearly perfected through the generations, do not try to make changes or apply the principle of another kind of exercise to it unless you have practiced the exercise for some time and have mastered its essence.

A healthy body is the vehicle of a healthy mind. Practice the exercises with constancy and you will be able to keep a healthy body. I wish you all the best.

Index

abdomen, xix, 30, 96
arteriosclerosis, xvii

back, 11, 29, 35, 37, 42–43, 46, 48, 51, 60, 65–66, 86, 94, 96, 105
backbone, 2, 8–9, 22, 26, 96
balance, xviii, 18
belly, xviii, 9, 33, 48, 96, 105
body movements, xviii, 1, 7, 94–95, 98, 107
bowels, 18
breathing methods, 1
breathing pattern, 1, 7, 16, 94
buttocks, 2, 22, 33, 38, 46, 50, 69, 89, 96

cervical vertebrae, 44, 53
chest, 2, 5, 9, 11–12, 16, 22, 35, 38, 60, 65–66, 80, 85, 87, 89, 94, 96, 99
chi, xiv, xvi, 17–19, 94–95, 97–98
chin, 2, 16, 22, 33, 94, 96
circular movement, 95, 106
circulatory system, 38, 46

dantian, xviii–xix, 7, 12, 22, 25, 32–33, 56, 75, 94–98
Daoyin, xv
depression, 5, 14
digestive system, xvii, 15, 18, 41
dizziness, 5, 14
doctor, xvii

Index

elbow, 10–11, 16, 37, 60, 82, 84, 87, 89, 95, 98–99, 101
exertion, xvi, xix, 11, 32, 45, 56, 58, 67, 77, 93
eye, 16, 20, 25, 28–29, 44–46, 56, 67, 93–94, 96–97

face, 4, 11–13, 34, 42, 63, 97, 99, 102, 104
fatigue, xvi, 20, 35, 43–44, 77
finger, 4, 23, 25–26, 28, 36, 42, 56, 78, 80, 84, 87, 89–90, 95, 97, 104
fist, 36, 45–46, 56–60, 62, 67–68
flexibility, xvi–xvii
forehead, 4, 12–13

head, xix, 2, 4–5, 12–13, 19–20, 26, 28, 30, 42, 50–51, 53, 69, 93–94, 96–97, 106
headache, 14
health, xiii–xv, xviii, 1, 55, 94
health improvement, xvii
heart, 9, 11
hypertension, xvii, 5, 14
hypotension, 5, 14

insomnia, 18
internal force, 45, 56, 58, 67, 77
internal organs, xv, 18, 30–31, 35, 41, 53, 96
internal physical balance, xvii

knee, 63, 65, 73, 84, 89, 105–106
kung fu, xvi

ligaments, 15, 35, 53, 77
limb, 7, 48
lower back, 11, 46
lumbago, 18

martial arts, xv–xvii, 21, 31, 55, 94
massage, xix, 30
meditation, 15, 21
mental, xvii–xviii, 2, 5, 16, 32
middle finger, 36, 42, 95
mind, xiii, xiv, xix, 2, 15–16, 22, 25, 27, 33, 56, 93–95, 107
mouth, 16, 22, 33, 94
muscle, xv, xvii–xviii, 15–16, 30–31, 35, 38, 41, 44, 46, 77

navel, xix, 2, 16, 22, 24, 95–96, 102, 105
neck, 2, 15, 20, 43–44, 94, 96
nervous system, 44, 46, 51, 96
nose, 2, 16, 22, 24, 27, 29, 33, 95–96
numbness, 7, 77

palate, 16, 27, 33, 94, 96
physical, xiv–xix, 21, 94
pregnant, xvii

Qigong, xviii

relaxation exercise, 51, 91
respiration, 93, 107
respiratory system, 9, 24
routine, 32, 55–56, 75, 91, 94, 107

self–discipline, xiii
Shaolin, 21, 31
shoulder, 2–4, 6, 8, 10, 16–17, 19,
    22, 25, 33, 36, 41, 45, 50, 82, 84,
    86, 89, 95–96, 98, 100–102, 104
sight, 94, 101, 104
spine, 15, 48, 50–51, 53, 95–96
spirit, xiii–xvi, 93–94
stamina, 46, 55
strength, xiv–xv, xvii–xix, 46, 93–94

Tai Chi Chuan, xiii, xvii, 7, 77, 93–95
teeth, 16, 22, 29, 33, 46, 56, 94, 96
tendon, xv, xvii, 11, 21, 31–32
tension, xvi, 51, 77, 94–95
thumb, 80, 82, 84, 87, 90

tongue, 16, 27, 33, 94, 96
torso, 2, 5, 17–18, 22, 30, 33, 45, 58,
    63, 73, 83, 86, 89, 103
traditional Chinese fitness exercises,
    xiii–xiv, 1, 21, 31

visualization, xiii, 107

waist, 43, 45, 65, 67, 78, 80, 86, 94,
    99–100
weariness, 35
wushu, 31

Yi Jin Jing, 21
yin and yang, xiv, xvi
Yoga, xviii

BOOKS OF RELATED INTEREST FROM NAB

CHINESE MASSAGE MANUAL — *Sarah Pritchard*
Chinese massage therapy has been practised for over 4,000 years. In China, where it is called 'Tui Na', it is still one of the most popular forms of treatment for a wide range of complaints. Safe, holistic and effective, Tui Na is a unique blend of hands-on massage technique with the principles of Chinese medicine. *The Chinese Massage Manual* includes everything you need to start practising on your friends and family. Follow the clear step-by-step instructions, refer to the theory charts and you will find the power of Chinese medicine at your fingertips!

ISBN: 81-7822-122-5

THE CHINESE WAY TO HEALTH: A Self-help Guide to Traditional Chinese Medicine — *Dr. Stephen Gascoigne*
Health has been described as our greatest gift—after all, everyone wants to know how to keep in the best state of health and well-being. Western medicine, while excelling at treating life-threatening diseases, traumatic injury and crisis intervention, falls far short of understanding or effectively treating chronic disease and degeneration. This is where Chinese medicine comes into play. Chinese medicine has a unique view of the whole person as an energetic network of interconnecting channels and organs.

ISBN: 81-7822-160-8

PRACTICAL GUIDE TO THE I CHING — *Kim-Anh lim*
Kim-Anh Lim gives a comprehensive overview of the *I Ching's* evolution in Chinese history and philosophy, and explains how to cast and interpret the hexagrams. She also includes complete interpretations, based on her exceptional insight into the ancient text, for each hexagram and its "changing" lines. This book holds a wealth of information. Kim-Anh Lim takes you step by step through the components of the hexagrams so you can better interpret how the hexagrams you cast for yourself apply to your particular situation.

ISBN: 81-7822-108-x

THE CHINESE HERBALIST'S HANDBOOK: A Practitioner's Reference Guide to Traditional Chinese Herbs and Formulas — *Dagmar Ehling*
Within the context of Oriental medicine, Chinese herbal medicine is one of the oldest treatment modalities. Though it is not as well known in the West, it is rapidly gaining popularity. China has achieved full integration of traditional Chinese and Western medicine and practitioners are usually trained in both practices. Patients are cross-referred on a continuous basis; they view both types of medicines as complementary, consulting one form of medicine for certain ailments, the other for different ones, or using both styles concurrently.

ISBN: 81-7822-196-9

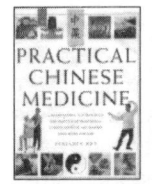

PRACTICAL CHINESE MEDICINE: Understanding the Principles and Practice of Traditional Chinese Medicine and Making them Work for You — *Penelope Ody*
Take a holistic approach to your health and discover the ancient art of Chinese medicine which is effective even today. Chinese medicine aims to cure diseases by focusing on the person and the cause, and identifying a range of highly detailed syndromes with specific treatment programmes. It will help you to discover the key to total health and heal yourself and your family of a wide range of common ailments: from allergies to insomnia making you aware of the Chinese diagnostic techniques.

ISBN: 81-7822-123-3

STRETCH YOUR LIMBS FOR BALANCE : Yoga for Long and Healthy Living — *Elise Browning Miller Carol Blackman*
This book shows you how to look younger, have more energy, and reduce stress with focused breathing, easy stretches, and relaxation techniques. Based on yoga principles, these simple techniques can be used anytime by people of all ages and ability levels. •Improve your ability to concentrate and think clearly • Burn fat and firm thighs, legs, and abdomen • Improve posture, flexibility, and strength • Restore calm and release stress • Strengthen your lower back and relieve sciatic pain.

ISBN: 81-7822-132-2

PRANAYAMA: A Conscious Way of Breathing — *Ranjit Sen Gupta*
Pranayama is the conscious perception and guidance of life energies which unfold self in complex forms in the psycho-physical system of all living beings. This book is for readers living in the modern world of high-tech environment and lifestyle, and searching for a soothing opposite pole. A deep and steady breathing consciously done for at least few minutes, brings relief and relaxation. This is a simple act of Pranayama. The book introduces us intelligently to the basic breathing practices and describes the fundamental aspects of their psycho-physiology.

ISBN: 81-7822-083-0

STEP-BY-STEP YOGA FOR STRESS RELIEF — *Swami Shivapremananda*
Yoga provides the perfect way to counteract the daily stresses that pervade both mind and body. Clearly and authoritatively written, with step-by-step illustrated instructions, *Yoga for Stress Relief* demonstrates yoga positions (asanas), breathing exercises (pranayamas) and meditations.
The book comprises of: A unique 3-month programme for de-stressing and stress prevention • Treatments for stress-related dis-orders, from migraine and asthma to anxiety and depression • Protection from emotional illness • Guidance for yoga in pregnancy and old age.

ISBN: 81-7822-046-6

THAI MASSAGE MANUAL : Natural Therapy for Flexibility, Relaxation and Energy Balance — *Maria Mercati*
Stay relaxed and healthy through the healing power of touch! One of the most ancient healing arts, Thai massage has worked wonders for centuries. By pressing, pulling, stretching, and manipulating the body, you'll affect both the joints and the soft tissues, improve flexibility, alleviate pain, increase vitality, and offer a completely pleasurable, relaxing experience. And you will enjoy it as much as the recipient. In fact, no other type of massage provides a more powerful combination of two people's energies.

ISBN: 81-7822-222-1

THE HEALING POWER OF YOGA — *Julie Friedeberger*
This is a book about yoga, a holistic system for creating and sustaining balance and harmony on all the levels of our being: body, mind, emotions and spirit. It's about yoga's boundless potential for healing, for bringing about beneficial change on all these levels. It's about how yoga can serve us as a source of inner strength in times of stress and difficulty, and in times of acute crisis, too: serious illness, bereavement, divorce, loss of job and income—the things we hope will never happen to us, but which do happen to most of us. For thousands of years, people who practise yoga have experienced the unfolding of awareness, self-discipline, stability, resilience and detachment—the inner resources that enable us to meet these challenges and to overcome the obstacles that life puts in our path.

ISBN: 81-7822-181-0